The best cute cats coloring book for adults

Thank you very much for buying this book if you like it please leave a review
Sincerely
Wilcher Eagle

COLPITUS

www.ingramcontent.com/pod-product-compliance
Lightning Source LLC
Chambersburg PA
CBHW081451250726
48662CB00009B/3043